PRESENTED TO

FROM

DATE

Poems for Easter

INSPIRING THOUGHTS

IDEALS PUBLICATIONS INCORPORATED
NASHVILLE, TENNESSEE

ISBN 0-8249-4174-8

Printed and bound by R. R. Donnelly & Sons in Mexico.
Library of Congress Cataloging-in-Publication Data on file.

POEMS SELECTED BY THORUNN RUGA MCCOY
DESIGNED BY EVE DEGRIE
EDITED BY ELIZABETH BONNER KEA

10 8 6 4 2 1 3 5 7 9

Published by Ideals Publications Incorporated
535 Metroplex Drive, Suite 250
Nashville, Tennessee 37211

ACKNOWLEDGMENTS

Ideals Publications Incorporated has made every effort to trace the ownership of all copyrighted material. Thanks are due to the following authors, publishers, and agents for permission to use the material indicated: COATSWORTH, ELIZABETH. "The Sun Comes Dancing." Reprinted by permission of Katherine Barnes. DAY, MYRTLE BEELER. "Resurrection." Used by permission of Lakeview United Methodist Church. DEVLIN, DENIS. "Ascension" from *Denis Devlin: Collected Poems*, ed. JCC Mays. Reprinted with permission of Wake Forest University Press. DICKINSON, EMILY. "A lady red amid the hill." Reprinted with permission of the publishers and the Trustees of Amherst College from *The Poems of Emily Dickinson*, Thomas H. Johnson, ed., Cambridge, Mass.: The Belknap Press of Harvard University Press, Copyright © 1951, 1955, 1979, 1983 by the President and Fellows of Harvard College. FARJEON, ELEANOR. "Morning Has Broken." Reprinted by permission of Harold Ober Associates Incorporated. Copyright 1951 by Eleanor Farjeon, copyright renewed. STEVENS, RUTH. "Easter Prayer" from *The Christian Home* by Ruth W. Stevens. Used by permission of Abingdon Press. WIDDEMER, MAR-GARET. "A Child's Easter Song." Used by permission of John D. Widdemer. Our sincere thanks to the following authors whom we were unable to locate: Louise Abney for "Easter Morning," Katharine Tynan Hinkson for "Love at Easter," Edgar Daniel Kramer for "He Is Risen!" and Claude McKay for "The Easter Flower."

Buds, ye will soon be flowers,
Cherry and white;
Snowstorms are changing to showers,
Darkness to light.
With the waking of spring,
Oh, sweetly sing—
"Lo! Christ the Lord is risen."
—EMILY D. CHAPMAN

*F*aith and hope triumphant say,
Christ will rise on Easter Day.

—PHILLIPS BROOKS

MORNING HAS BROKEN

Morning has broken like the first morning;
Blackbird has spoken like the first bird.
Praise for the singing! Praise for the morning!
Praise for them springing fresh from the Word.

Sweet the rain's new fall, sunlit from heaven,
Like the first dewfall on the first grass.
Praise for the sweetness of the wet garden,
Sprung in completeness where His feet pass.

Mine is the sunlight, mine is the morning,
Born of the one light Eden saw play.
Praise with elation, praise every morning,
God's recreation of the new day.

—ELEANOR FARJEON

THE SUN COMES DANCING

On Easter morn,
  On Easter morn,
    The Sun comes dancing up the sky.

    His light leaps up;
It shakes and swings,
Bewildering the dazzled eye.

On Easter morn,
All earth is glad;
The waves rejoice in the bright sea.

Be still and listen
To your heart,
And hear it beating merrily!
—ELIZABETH COATSWORTH

LOVE AT EASTER

Sing to the Lord a new song!
Because the spring comes newly,
And every slender sapling
Has budded green and red.
Sing to the Lord a new song!
The skylark sings it truly,
Since all in dewy April
His love and he are wed.

Sing to the Lord a new song!
For every bird's a lover,
And o'er the purple furrows
The green spears nod and wave.
Sing to the Lord a new song!
Since Lenten fasts are over,
And Easter's come in glory,
And Christ has left the grave.

—KATHARINE TYNAN HINKSON

The same power that brought Christ back from the dead is operative within those who are Christ's. The Resurrection is an ongoing thing.—LEON MORRIS

EASTER

Easter, with its voice of Spring,
Ushers in the morning;
'Tis time for earth's awakening,
Time for earth's adorning.

Let church bells sound their chimes
And ring out on the air,

A call to come to worship
And meet the Lord in prayer.

With heart and love ascending,
Your joyful praises sing,
In faith and hope and wonder—
Behold your risen King!

—INEZ LEMKE

Resurrection is there for us to witness and participate in; but the resurrection around us still remains the symbol, not the ultimate truth.—HAL BORLAND

DAWN

I love the dawn, the gentle light of morning,
When diamonds of the sky grow dim
And golden sun sneaks o'er the brim,
The newborn day adorning.

As dawn shall break, the songbird's joyful singing
Blends with the beauty of the light
To start another day just right,
A new hope always bringing.

Another day, thank God for glorious dawn,
Which fades the darkness of the night
And gives new faith and clearer sight
That our hearts may carry on.
—W. EARLINGTON WHITNEY

For the flower glorifies God.
—CHRISTOPHER SMART

AN EASTER GREETING

The lark at sunrise trills it high—
The greeting Christ is risen!
And through the wood the blackbird pipes
The greeting Christ is risen!
Beneath the eaves the swallows cry
The greeting Christ is risen!
Throughout the world man's heart proclaims
The greeting Christ is risen!
And echo answers from the grave
In truth, yes, He is risen!

—MAIKOW

Jesus is risen! He shall the world restore!
Awake, ye dead, dull sinners, sleep no more!
—JOHN WESLEY

*G*od laughs in the sunshine and rejoices in the songs of the springtime birds.—BRUCE BARTON

THE MESSAGE

Easter morning brings a message;
We can sense it in the air.
We can see it in the sunrise;
It is waiting everywhere.

Oh, the beauty of the lilies!
It is there if we but look,
And we feel it in the dewdrops,
Hear it in the rushing brook.

Chiming bells reiterate it,
Ring the message far and wide;
Keeping measure with the heartbeat,
Bringing joy we cannot hide.

And we find it in the faces
That we meet along the way.
They shine with an inner radiance;
They smile in a different way.

Yes, it greets us with the morning,
No more need to search and grope;
It is there for all to cherish,
Easter's precious message—hope.

—VILETA CHASE

Let us live with our faces turned toward the rising sun—the risen Son.—S. D. GORDON

GODMINSTER CHIMES

O chime of sweet Saint Charity, peal soon that Easter morn
When Christ for all shall risen be, and in all hearts new-born.
That Pentecost when utterance clear to all men shall be given,
When all shall say *My Brother* here, and hear *My Son* in heaven!
—JAMES LOWELL

To me it seems as if when God conceived the
world, that was poetry.—EMMA STEBBINS

Precious as are all the seasons of the
year, none so rejoices the heart as spring.
There is about spring a gladness that
thrills the soul and lifts it up into regions
of spiritual sunshine.—HELEN KELLER

AN EASTER MORN

Brightly now the sun is shining
On this Easter Sabbath morn:
Voices heavenward are inclining;
And the sky's without a scorn.

Beautiful white clouds are moving
'Cross the broad expanse of blue
Which o'erhangs the earth, so soothing,
Reflecting its azure hue.

In the ponds, the streams and rivers,
Lending color to their depth.
In the breeze the dead grass quivers
As if it received fresh breath.

—CHARLES FREDERICK WHITE

EASTER

No human eye was by
To witness Christ arise,
But I, this morning heard
The Resurrection of the Word.

It sprang through night, opaque,
A note so pure and clear,
I felt my spirit wake—
It flooded everywhere.

I know that is has been;
There is a vision new.
I see the universe
Divinely bathed in dew.

—SISTER MARY AGNES

And in the green underwood and cover, blossom by blossom
the spring begins. —ALGERNON CHARLES SWINBURNE

But yonder comes the powerful King of Day,
rejoicing in the east. —JAMES THOMSON

EASTER DAY

Oh, Easter anthems gladly sing,
Let all the bells from towers ring,
And sun dispel with brightening rays
The darkness of the Passion days!
Fair lilies with their crystal light
And eager, joyous greetings bright
Proclaim the Lord has risen again,
And put asunder death and pain!
—JOSEPHINE RICE CREELMAN

EIGHTEEN

BELLS OF ST. MICHAEL

On the gladsome Easter morning,
When the earliest flowerets bloom,
Snowdrops pure and violets purple
Blend to scatter sweet perfume;
Then your happiest notes are poured forth,
Then your Jubilee is heard,
Pealing out in joyful accents,
Chiming, "God is very good."

Dear old bells your music thrills me,
Whether run in joy or woe,
They recall the joyous spring time
Of fond memory's "long ago."
Sweetly chime through all the ages;
As time's cycles swiftly move;
Peal forth loudly, "God is gracious!"
Whisper softly, "He is love."
—MARY WESTON FORDHAM

Heaven and earth, and saints and friends and flowers
are keeping Easter Day!—AUTHOR UNKNOWN

This Easter sun will rise on you, dear child, feeling your "life in every
limb," and eager to rush out into the fresh morning air.—LEWIS CARROLL

EASTER MORNING

Pines whose whispers fill the air, birches bowed as if in prayer,
Benedictions everywhere on Easter Morning.

On the mountain's azure crest, far above the placid breast
Of the lake are clouds at rest on Easter Morning.

Butterflies and birds and bees, altar-hills, and singing trees,
Faith is born of things like these on Easter Morning.
—LOUISE ABNEY

Nothing is without voice; God everywhere can hear
Arising from creation His praise and echo clear. —ANGELUS SILESIUS

DAWN ANTHEMS

In my garden this morning
Beauty reigned supreme;
I saw each chaliced lily
Waken from her dream.

The dew had washed their faces;
They sparkled with delight.

Their gowns shimmered with stardust,
Left over from last night.

Dawn was robed in rose and gold,
And I heard the woodbirds sing
Anthems of adoration
To Christ the risen King.

—RUTH POWELL SINGER

*E*aster proclaims that man shall overcome all his foes, including death itself. His pathway may lead him through the sorrows of Gethsemane, the pain and darkness of Calvary, nevertheless his winter of distress will yet turn to the spring of delight.—CHARLES E. HESSELGRAVE

FOR EASTER MORN

How gladly dawns the Easter sun!
The wide world thrills with prayer and praise.
Gone by are all Lent's mournful days,
And Hope and Joy seem just begun.

The laughing streams to seaward run—
Wild flowers bedeck the woodland ways,
And homing birds sing merry lays
Of triumph over winter done.

Shall we not joy? We, too, have won,
Through winter's hostile ice-bound days,
To this new dawn that all things praise;
Let us be glad—aye, every one—
When gladly dawns the Easter sun.

—LOUISE CHANDLER MOULTON

EASTER DAWN

This is the pattern of the day I sought:
Soft rains to woo the early buds to flower,
With hope renewed as greater faith is wrought,
While sacred beauty fills the holy hour.

With ceasing rain to watch a new sun rise,
Shedding its brilliance with each golden ray—
Clouds rolling back, as true and nature-wise
As did the stone on that triumphant day.

And then to hear again God say to man:
This is my hope and resurrection plan.
—MAY SMITH WHITE

*J*esus' rising is an Easter, a dawn, the dawn of day for mankind,
and for the earth.—S. D. GORDON

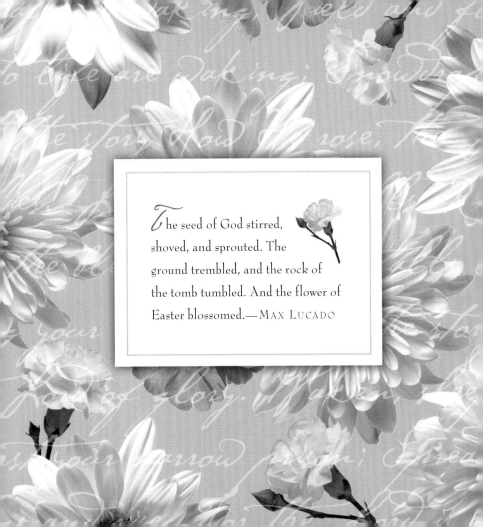

The seed of God stirred, shoved, and sprouted. The ground trembled, and the rock of the tomb tumbled. And the flower of Easter blossomed.—MAX LUCADO

THE EASTER FLOWER

Far from this foreign Easter, damp and chilly,
My soul steals to a pear-shaped plot of ground
Where gleamed the lilac-tinted Easter Lily
Soft-scented in the air for yards around;

Alone, without a hint of guardian leaf,
Just like a fragile bell of silver rime,
It burst the tomb for freedom sweet and brief
In the young, pregnant year at Eastertime;

And many thought it was a sacred sign,
And some called it the resurrection flower;
And I, in wonder, worshiped at its shrine,
Yielding my heart unto its perfumed power.

—CLAUDE MCKAY

AT EASTER TIME

The little flowers came through the ground,
At Eastertime, at Eastertime;
They raised their heads and looked around,
At happy Eastertime.
And every pretty bud did say,
"Good people bless this holy day,
For Christ is risen, the angels say
At happy Eastertime!"

The pure white lily raised its cup,
At Eastertime, at Eastertime;
The crocus to the sky looked up
At happy Eastertime.
"We'll hear the song of Heaven!" they say,
"Its glory shines on us today.
Oh! may it shine on us always
At holy Eastertime."

'Twas long and long and long ago,
That Eastertime, that Eastertime;
But still the pure white lilies blow
At happy Eastertime.
And still each little flower doth say,
"Good Christians, bless this holy day,
For Christ is risen, the angels say
At blessed Eastertime."
—LAURA E. RICHARDS

The lilies say: Behold how we preach, without words, of purity.—CHRISTINA ROSSETTI

NATURE'S EASTER MUSIC

The flowers from the earth have arisen,
They are singing their Easter song;
Up the valleys and over the hillsides
They come, an unnumbered throng.

Oh listen! The wildflowers are singing
Their beautiful songs without words!
They are pouring the soul of their music
Through the voices of happy birds.

Every flower to a bird has confided
The joy of its blossoming birth—
The wonder of its resurrection
From its grave in the frozen earth.

The buttercup's thanks for the sunshine
The goldfinch's twitter reveals;

And the violet trills, through the bluebird,
Of the heaven that within her she feels.

The song-sparrow's exquisite warble
Is born in the heart of the rose—
Of the wild-rose, shut in its calyx,
Afraid of belated snows.
—LUCY LARCOM

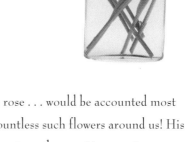

A man who could make one rose . . . would be accounted most
wonderful; yet God scatters countless such flowers around us! His
gifts are so infinite that we do not see them.—MARTIN LUTHER

EASTER SONG

Snowdrops, lift your timid heads,
All the earth is waking;
Field and forest, brown and dead,
Into life are waking.
Snowdrops, rise and tell the story
How He rose, the Lord of glory.

Lilies! Lilies! Easter calls,
Rise to meet the dawning
Of the blessed light that falls

Through the Easter morning;
Ring your bells and tell the story,
How He rose, the Lord of glory.

Waken, sleeping butterflies,
Burst your narrow prison;
Spread your golden wings and rise,
For the Lord is risen.
Spread your wings and tell the story,
How He rose, the Lord of glory.

—MARY A. LATHBURY

*E*very revelation of truth felt with interior savor
and spiritual joy is a sacred whispering of God in the
ear of a pure soul.—WALTER HILTON

*T*he Lord has turned all our sunsets into sunrises.

—CLEMENT OF ALEXANDRIA

University Christian School
Media Center

EASTER FLOWERS

Easter flowers are blooming bright;
Easter skies pour radiant light;
Christ our Lord is risen in might,
Glory in the highest.

Angels caroled this sweet lay
When in manger rude He lay;
Now once more cast grief away,
Glory in the highest.

He, then born to grief and pain,
Now to glory born again,
Calleth forth our gladdest strain,
Glory in the highest.

As He riseth, rise we too,
Tune we heart and voice anew,
Offering homage glad and true,
Glory in the highest.

—MARY A. NICHOLSON

Earth, with her thousand voices, praises God.—SAMUEL TAYLOR COLERIDGE

For the flowers are great blessings.—CHRISTOPHER SMART

EASTER

Unfolding of the lilies,
The singing of the birds
Tell of the joys of Easter
Better than we in words.

That peace and love triumphant
Over all the earth shall be—
This resurrection message
Is brought to you and me.
—ISABELLE CARTER YOUNG

THE LILIES

"Look to the lilies how they grow!"
'Twas thus the Saviour said, that we,
Even in the simplest flowers that blow,
God's ever-watchful care might see.
—DAVID MOIR

RESURGAM

Lo, now comes the April pageant
And the Easter of the year.
Now the tulip lifts her chalice,
And the hyacinth his spear;
All the daffodils and jonquils
With their hearts of gold are here.
Child of the immortal vision,
What has thou to do with fear?

When the summons wakes the impulse,
And the blood beats in the vein,
Let no grief thy dream encumber,
No regret thy thought detain.
Through the scented bloom-hung valleys,
Over tillage, wood, and plain,
Comes the soothing south wind laden
With the sweet impartial rain.

All along the roofs and pavements
Pass the volleying silver showers,
To unfold the hearts of humans
And the frail unanxious flowers.
Breeding fast in sunlit places,
Teeming life puts forth her powers,
And the migrant wings come northward
On the trail of golden hours.

Over intervale and upland
Sounds the robin's interlude
From his tree-top spire at evening
Where no unbeliefs intrude.
Every follower of beauty
Finds in the spring solitude
Sanctuary and persuasion
Where the mysteries still brood.
—BLISS CARMAN

*Flowers may beckon
towards us, but they speak
toward heaven and God.*
—HENRY WARD BEECHER

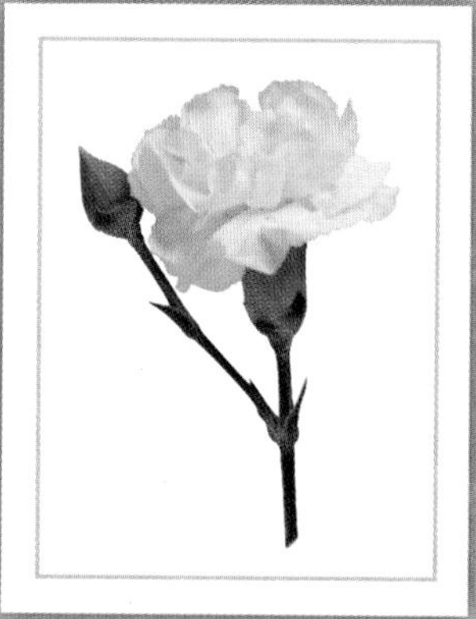

THE LILY'S MESSAGE

The Easter lily blooms again
From out the deep dark sod;
Its snowy bells bring messages
With every graceful nod.

The lily speaks of purity,
Of faith and trust and love;
It bids us to be grateful for
Each blessing from above.

It speaks of everlasting life
That came from out the tomb,

Upon that far-off Easter morn
When Christ cast off death's gloom.

To walk again with those He loved,
To touch the fragrant flowers
That grew within the garden walls,
To spend more happy hours

With those who had believed Him dead,
Who mourned Him as one gone,
The lily bids us greet Him now,
This blessed Easter dawn.

—MARIE ELMORE BAXTER

My soul is linked right tenderly to every shady copse;
I prize the creeping violet.—ELIZA COOK

RESURRECTION DAY

When jonquils break the earthly crust,
Where winter winds have blown,
To bloom in all their glory,
Awakening with the dawn;
When tulips that lay dormant,
Rise up through straw-clad beds;
And violets and dandelions
Wake up and lift their heads;

When morning glories climb the fence,
And birds new houses make,
Then the time is drawing near
For a sleeping world to wake,
For trees to burst their swelling boughs
And garnish the world with green,

And the resurrection of the morning sun
To bring the loveliest day yet seen.

The Easter lilies so snowy white
With purity seem to say,
"The borrowed tomb is empty,
And the stone is rolled away."
The spring, through the countless ages,
Will its Easter message bring;
And the newness of life comes once again
Through the rising of the King.
—ANNIE LAURIE DUNAWAY

Easter is a constant spring.—RUTH CARRINGTON

THE CROCUS FLAME

The Easter sunrise flung a bar of gold
O'er the awakening world.
What was thine answer, O thou brooding earth?
What token of rebirth,
  Of tender vernal mirth,
    Thou, the long-prisoned in the bonds of cold?
    Under the kindling panoply which God
    Spreads over tree and clod,
I looked far abroad.
Under the sodden reaches seamed and sere
As when the dying year,
With rime-white sandals shod,
Faltered and fell upon its frozen bier.
Of some wraith quickening, some divine
Renaissance not a sign!
And yet, and yet,
With touch of viol-chord, with mellow fret,

The lyric South amid the bough-tops stirred,
And one lone bird an unexpected jet
Of song projected through the morning blue,
As though some wondrous hidden thing it knew.
And so I gathered heart, and cried again:
"O earth, make plain, at this matutinal hour,
The triumph and the power
Of life eternal over death and pain,
Although it be but by some simple flower!"
And then, with sudden light
Was dowered my veiled sight,
And I beheld in a sequestered place
A slender crocus show its sun-bright face.
O miracle of Grace,
Earth's Easter answer came,
The revelation of transfiguring Might,
In that small crocus flame!
—CLINTON SCOLLARD

RESURRECTION

The promise of resurrection
Is not only told in the Book;
It is heralded in the springtime
By every gurgling brook.

It is announced by violets
And by the dogwood trees.
It is changed by the mockingbird
And the buzzing of the bees.

It is echoed every Easter
By the lily's perfumed breath,
When every sleeping plant awakes,
Triumphant over death.

—EMILY MAY YOUNG

RESURRECTION OF HOPE

How beautiful are the greening hills
And pastures lying in between.
Wildflowers are blooming everywhere
And trees put on new leaves of green.
Up over all this varied hue
Lies a canopy of blue.

Spring is a birth time for the world—
A resurrection of new hope.

—AGNES DAVENPORT BOND

For flowers are peculiarly the poetry
of Christ.—CHRISTOPHER SMART

God is giving us the Easter flowers in little hidden nooks in the forests, down by the corners of fences, in the sheltered places on the edges of the brook; and there we find the violet, the arbutus and other delicate blossoms which lead the van for the great army of nature's efflorescence.—MARGARET SANGSTER

THE LILY OF THE RESURRECTION

While the lily dwells in the earth,
Walled about with crumbling mold,
She the sacred of her birth
Guesses not, nor has been told.

Hides the brown bulb in the ground,
Knowing not she is a flower;
Knowing not she shall be crowned
As a queen, with white-robed power.

Though her whole life is one thrill
Upward, unto skies unseen,
In her husks she wraps her still,
Wondering what her visions mean.

Shivering, while the bursting scales
Leave her heart bare, with a sigh
She her unclad state bewails,
Whispering to herself, "I die."

Die? Then may she welcome death,
Leaving darkness underground,
Breathing out her sweet, free breath
Into the new heavens around.

Die? She bathes in ether warm:
Beautiful without, within,
See at last the imprisoned form
All its fair proportions win!

Life it means, this impulse high
Which through every rootlet stirs:
Lo! the sunshine and the sky
She was made for, now are hers.

Soul, thou too art set in earth,
Heavenward through the dark to grow:
Dreamest thou of thy royal birth?
Climb! and thou shalt surely know.

Shuddering Doubt to Nature cries—
Nature, though she smiles, is dumb—
"How then can the dead arise?
With what body do they come?"

Lo, the unfolding mystery!
We shall bloom, some wondrous hour,
As the lily blooms, when she
Dies a bulb, to live a flower.

—LUCY LARCOM

EASTER MORN

Say, Earth, why hast thou got thee new attire,
And stick'st thy habit full of daisies red?
Seems that thou dost to some high thought aspire,
And some new-found-out bridegroom mean'st to wed;
Tell me, ye trees, so fresh apparellèd,—
So never let the spiteful canker waste you,
So never let the heavens with lightning blast you—
Why go you now so trimly dressed, or whither haste you?
Ye primroses and purple violets,
Tell me, why blaze ye from your leavy bed,
And woo men's hands to rent you from your sets,
As though you would somewhere be carrièd,
With fresh perfumes, and velvets garnishèd?
But, ah! I need not ask, 'tis surely so,
You all would to your Saviour's triumphs go,
There would ye all await, and humble homage do.

—GILES FLETCHER

The Omnipotent has sown His name on the heavens in glittering stars, but upon earth He planteth His name by tender flowers.—JEAN PAUL RICHTER

Somehow Easter always carries with it more of heaven than any other of the great anniversaries of the Christian year.—MARGARET SANGSTER

AN EASTER WISH

All flowers blooming, bright and sweet,
In loveliness are so complete . . .
They seem to say in their own way,
"We wish you joy this Easter Day."
—RACHEL HARTNETT

RISE, FLOWERS, RISE

Little children of the sun,
Wake and listen, every one!
Hear the raindrops as they fall,
Hear the winds that call and call,
"Rise, flowers, rise!"

Children, little sleepy-heads,
It is time to leave your beds,
Snowdrop and hepatica,
Pink spring-beauty, lead the way;
"Rise, flowers, rise!"

Tell the grasses and the trees,
Tell the bluebirds and the bees,
Tell the ferns, like croziers curled,

It is Easter in the world,
"Rise, flowers, rise!"

Waken, tardy violets;
Waken, innocent bluets;
Waken, every growing thing,
It is Easter, it is spring!
"Rise, flowers, rise!"

Rise, for Christ the Lord arose,
Victor over all His foes;
Rise, with all the souls of men,
Into light and life again;
"Rise, flowers, rise!"
—MARY A. LATHBURY

Easter spells out beauty, the rare beauty of new life.—S. D. GORDON

ON EASTER DAY

Easter lilies! Can you hear
What they whisper, low and clear?
In dewy fragrance they unfold
Their splendor sweet, their snow and gold.
Every beauty-breathing bell
News of heaven has to tell.
Listen to their mystic voice,
Hear, oh mortal, and rejoice!
Hark, their soft and heavenly chime!
Christ is risen for all time!
—CELIA THAXTER

Christ Himself is living at the heart of the world: and His total mystery—
that of creation, incarnation, redemption, and resurrection—embodies and
animates all of life and all of history.—MICHEL QUOIST

𝒯was Easter Sunday. The
full-blossomed trees filled all the
air with fragrance and with joy.

—HENRY WADSWORTH LONGFELLOW

RESURRECTION

Lord, I cannot doubt
The resurrection
When spring is here,
And I witness the sight
Of bare apple trees
Miraculously turned
Into bridal bouquets
Of lovely white.

For I know that this
Transcendent power,
That could only come
From One Divine,
Which brings to life
Somnolent apple trees
Will, one day, resurrect
This body of mine.

—EARLE J. GRANT

Thus we come to Easter . . . celebrating life and hope and the ultimate substance of belief—reaching, like the leaf itself, for something beyond, ever beyond.—HAL BORLAND

RESURRECTION

The dark, bare branches
Of the pin oaks
Against the somber sky, gray still
With the chill of winter
Are fringed
With the misty, feathery green
Of spring.

My heart leaps
With the thought
Of the joy and beauty
Of the resurrection upon the earth,
Intimations in God's universe
Of immortality.

—MYRTLE BEELER DAY

*F*aith is the root; hope is the stem; love, the perfect flower. You may have faith without hope, and hope without love; but you cannot have love apart from faith and hope.—F. B. MEYER

LOVELIEST OF TREES,
THE CHERRY NOW

Loveliest of trees, the cherry now
Is hung with bloom along the bough,
And stands about the woodland ride
Wearing white for Eastertide.

Now, of my threescore years and ten,
Twenty will not come again,
And take from seventy springs a score,
It only leaves me fifty more.

And since to look at things in bloom
Fifty springs are little room,
About the woodlands I will go
To see the cherry hung with snow.

—A. E. HOUSMAN

SYMBOLS OF EASTERTIME

Each tiny bud on naked trees
And seedlings bursting 'neath the ground,
The babbling brooks which sing with glee
Are symbols of our Eastertime.

The wide blue heavens, crystal clear,
Snow ball clouds with ribboned lace,
The flaming sun, a golden throne,
Are symbols of our Eastertime.

The trilling birds in search of love,
And raindrop tears that thirst the land:
The whispering winds, their lullabyes
Are symbols of our Eastertime.

The faith, the hope in Jesus, Lord
Who died and gave His life for us,
Then rose to heaven to be with God
Gives meaning to our Eastertime.

—GERTRUDE RUDBERG

When the oak is felled, the whole forest echoes with its fall, but a hundred acorns are sown in silence by an unnoticed breeze.—THOMAS CARLYLE

FIFTY-FIVE

THE AWAKENING

You little, eager, peeping thing—
You embryonic point of light
Pushing from out your winter night,
How you do make my pulses sing!

A tiny eye amid the gloom—
The merest speck I scarce had seen—
So doth God's rapture rend the tomb
In this wee burst of April green!

And lo, 'tis here, and lo 'tis there,
Spurting its jets of sweet desire
In upward curling threads of fire
Like tapers kindling all the air.

Why, scarce it seems an hour ago
These branches clashed in bitter cold;
What Power hath set their veins aglow?
O soul of mine, be bold, be bold!

If from this tree, this blackened thing,
Hard as the floor my feet have pressed,
This flame of joy comes clamoring
In hues as red as robin's breast
Waking to life this little twig—
O faith of mine, be big, be big!

—Angela Morgan

We see God all around us: the mountains are God's thoughts upheaved; the rivers are God's thoughts in motion; the oceans are God's thoughts imbedded; the dewdrops are God's thoughts in pearls.—SAM JONES

God! sing ye, meadow-streams, with gladsome voice,
Ye pine groves, with your soft and soul-like sounds.
—SAMUEL TAYLOR COLERIDGE

ON EASTER SUNDAY

'Twas Easter Sunday.
The full-blossomed trees
Filled all the air with
Fragrance and joy.
—HENRY WADSWORTH LONGFELLOW

EASTER IN THE WOODS

This dawn when the mountain cherry lifts
Its frail white bloom among dark pines,
And chipmunks flash small happy paws
Along old tumbled boundary lines,
This golden morning when the vixen
Nuzzles her five young foxes forth
To roll in ferns in the Easter sun,
Again the woods know soft green birth.
Snuffed by a puffball infant rabbit
Are yellow violets by the spring;
Among half-opened apple buds
A wood thrush tilts its head to sing.
Risen is He! And they are His
Who scamper under warm blue skies,
Who nibble little fists of grass,
And gaze on the earth with glad eyes.
—FRANCES FROST

Nature awakes and reechoes in springtime.—LIONEL BRUCE KINGERY

The world is charged with the grandeur of God.
—GERARD MANLEY HOPKINS

EASTER EVEN

You sleeping buds, break open your green cerements, and wake
To fragrant blossoming for His sweet sake; tomorrow will be Easter Day.
You home-bound birds, take swift-winged flight, that from my budding brake
Your joyful hallelujahs you may make; tomorrow will be Easter Day.
—MARGARET FRENCH PATTON

But more than just the sprouting of seed and bulblet brave, Easter ends
the doubting of life beyond the grave.—ENOLA CHAMBERLIN

*S*pring bursts today, for Christ is risen and all the earth's at play.

—CHRISTINA ROSSETTI

THE WAKING YEAR

A lady red amid the hill
Her annual secret keeps;
A lady white within the field
In placid lily sleeps.

The tidy breezes with their brooms
Sweep vale, and hill, and tree;
Prithee, my pretty housewives,
Who may expected be?

The neighbors do not yet suspect,
The woods exchange a smile—
Orchard, and buttercup, and bird—
In such a little while.

And yet how still the landscape stands,
How nonchalant the hedge,
As if the Resurrection
Were nothing very strange!

—EMILY DICKINSON

God's promises are kept. O soul, why not look out and sing:
"My God is Life, and Life is mine, sweet certainty of spring!"
—ETHEL COLWELL SMITH

SPRING

Observe God in His works: here fountains flow,
Birds sing, beast feed, fish leap, and the earth stands fast.
Above are restless motions, running lights,
Vast circling azure, giddy clouds, days, nights.
—HENRY VAUGHAN

THE SPARROW

When Jesus hung upon the cross
The birds, 'tis said, bewailed the loss
Of Him who first to mortals taught,
Guiding with love the life of all
And heeding e'en the sparrow's fall.
—CHARLES GODFREY LELAND

YE HEAVENS, UPLIFT YOUR VOICE

Ye heav'ns uplift your voice;
Sun, moon, and stars, rejoice
And thou, too, nether earth,
Join in the common mirth;

For winter storm at last,
And rain is over-past;
Instead whereof the green
And fruitful palm is seen.

Ye flow'rs of spring, appear,
Your gentle heads uprear,
And let the growing seed
Enamel lawn and mead.

Ye roses interset
With clumps of violet,
Ye lilies white, unfold
In beds of marigold.

Ye birds with open throat
Prolong your sweetest note;
Awake, ye blissful choirs,
And strike your merry lyres;

For why? Unhurt by death,
The Lord of Life and Breath,
Jesus, as He foresaid,
Is risen from the dead.

—FIFTEENTH-CENTURY CAROL

EASTER WEEK

See the land, her Easter keeping, rises as her Maker rose.
Seeds, so long in darkness sleeping, burst at last from winter snows.
Earth with heaven above rejoices, fields and gardens hail the spring;
Sloughs and woodlands ring with voices, while the wild birds build and sing.

You to whom your Maker granted powers to those sweet birds unknown,
Use the craft by God implanted; use the reason not your own.
Here, while heaven and earth rejoices, each his Easter tribute bring—
Work of fingers, chant of voices, like the birds who build and sing.

—CHARLES KINGSLEY

RESURRECTION

Then come, O fresh spring airs, once more
Create the old delightful things,
And woo the frozen world again
With hints of heaven upon your wings!

—HARRIET PRESCOTT SPOFFORD

AN EASTER CANTICLE

In every trembling bud and bloom
That cleaves the earth, a flowery sword,
I see Thee come from out the tomb,
Thou risen Lord.

In every April wind that sings
Down lanes that make the heart rejoice,
Yea, in the word the wood-thrush brings,
I hear Thy voice.
—CHARLES HANSON TOWNE

Springtime . . . invites you to try out its splendor . . . to
believe anew. To realize that the same Lord who renews the
trees with buds and blossoms is ready to renew your life with
hope and courage.—CHARLES R. SWINDOLL

EASTER, 1923

Once more the Ancient Wonder
Brings back the goose and crane,
Prophetic Sons of Thunder,
Apostles of the Rain.

In many a battling river
The broken gorges boom.
Behold, the Mighty Giver
Emerges from the tomb.

Now robins chant the story
Of how the wintry sward
Is lighted with the glory
Of the Angel of the Lord.

His countenance is lightning,
And still His robe is snow,
As when the dawn was brightening
Two thousand years ago.

O who can be a stranger
To what has come to pass?
The Pity of the Manger
Is mighty in the grass.

Undaunted by Decembers,
The sap is faithful yet.
The giving Earth remembers
And only men forget.

—John G. Neihardt

The holy spirit of the spring is working silently.—George MacDonald

$\mathcal{T}$hese as they change, Almighty Father, these are but the varied God. The rolling year is full of Thee.—JAMES THOMSON

EASTER PRAYER

We thank Thee, God, for spring. When earth turns green
And ice-freed streams play tinkling tunes. The chill
Wind blows no more, so blossoms bud. Between
Sun-stenciled leaves, the first shy warblers trill.

We thank Thee, God, for light and soft warm air;
For daffodils whose golden shine adorns
The tufted grass; for woods where hilltops wear
Blue violets for crown instead of thorns.

We thank, Thee, God, for life. Now spring is here—
Revive in us fresh understanding, give
New wisdom for the tasks ahead, melt fear
With love—You gave Your Son that we might live.

Dear God, as spring and life return again,
Accept the thanks of grateful hearts. Amen.
—RUTH W. STEVENS

$\mathcal{E}$very April God rewrites the book of Genesis. — AUTHOR UNKNOWN

EASTER

The air is like a butterfly
With frail blue wings.
The happy earth looks at the sky
And sings.

—JOYCE KILMER

$\mathcal{A}$ voice is in the wind I do not know; a meaning on the face of the high hills whose utterance I cannot comprehend. A something is behind them: that is God. — GEORGE MACDONALD

EASTER

You who fear death remember April
With her sword of jade
On a thousand hills,
And the warm south wind
That whispers
Of cornel and of purple squills.

You who fear death remember April
With her moon-white trees
And the new-turned sod,—
And the bare, brown branch
That quickens
Like a sudden thought of God.

—JOHN RICHARD MORELAND

EVOLUTION

Out of the dark a shadow,
Then, a spark;
Out of the cloud a silence,
Then, a lark;
Out of the heart a rapture,
Then, a pain;
Out of the dead cold ashes,
Life again.

—JOHN B. TABB

The world is very lovely,
O my God, I thank thee that I live!

—ALEXANDER SMITH

EASTER FLOWERS

Blooming to garland Easter, white as the drifted snows,
Are the beautiful vestal lilies, the myriad-petaled rose,
Carnations with hearts of fire, and the heather's fragrant spray—
Blooming to garland Easter, and strew our King's highway.

Late we had gloom and sorrow, but the word from Heaven forth
Has scattered the clouds before it like a trumpet blown from the north;
And east and west and southward the flowers arise today
To garland the blithesome Easter, and strew the King's highway.

—MARGARET E. SANGSTER

SEVENTY-TWO

THE MIRACLE OF SPRING

The miracle of spring may come
To any man on earth,
And tranquil thought may trill with
Life's abundant power and worth.

The sap climbs up. The tallest tip
Awakes in graceful glee,
For April's wholly unconcerned
With laws of gravity.

Fragrant flowers are loveliest
At close of winter storm.
O blessed fact: No fall seed died,
It grew and changed its form.

Then why art thou cast down, O soul,
Why not let hope hold sway?

For crucifixion always ends
In a resurrection day.

The hour is come for thee to live
As the son of God should live;
To satisfy the Christ within;
To know, and be, and give.

And should some boastful bluster
Corner thee in dusky tomb,
Three days good work will raise thee up;
Life needs a radiant room.

God's promises are kept, O soul,
Why not look out and sing:
"My God is Life, and Life is mine,
Sweet certainty of spring."

—ETHEL COLWELL SMITH

"HE IS RISEN!"

"He is risen!" Lo, the grasses
Fill the meadows with their mirth,
While the lilacs lift hosannas
As their fragrance thrills the earth.

"He is risen!" Lo, the birches
And the oaks high on the hills
Mingle their rejoicing chorus
With the songs of daffodils.

"He is risen!" Lo, the willows
Leaning where the waters run,
Tremulous, in adulation
Hymn the glory of God's Son.

"He is risen!" Lo, we harken
To the strangely mystic words,
That are filling us with rapture
In the minstrelsy of birds.

"He is risen"!" Lo, we echo
Adoration in our eyes,
As a host of shining angels
Fling glad songs across the skies.

"He is risen!" Lo, we worship,
Kneeling with each leaf and bloom,
While Lord Jesus leads the springtime
From the darkness of His tomb.

—EDGAR DANIEL KRAMER

THE REVIVAL

Unfold, unfold! take in His light,
Who makes thy cares more short than night.
The joys, which with His day-star rise,
He deals to all, but drowsy eyes:
And what the men of their world miss,
Some drops and dews of future bliss.

Hark how His winds have changed their note,
And with warm whispers call thee out.
The frosts are past, the storms are gone:
And backward life at last comes on.
The lofty groves express joys
Reply unto the turtle's voice,
    And here in dust and dirt, O here,
    The lilies of His love appear!
    —HENRY VAUGHAN

COMPOSED IN ONE OF THE VALLEYS
OF WESTMORELAND, ON EASTER SUNDAY

With each recurrence of this glorious morn
That saw the Saviour in His human frame
Rise from the dead, erewhile the cottage-dame
Put on fresh raiment—till that hour unworn:
Domestic hand the home-bred wool had shorn,
And she who spun it culled the daintiest fleece,
In thoughtful reverence to the Prince of Peace,
Whose temples bled beneath the platted thorn.
A blessed estate when piety sublime
These humble props disdained not! O green dales!
Sad may I be who heard your sabbath chime
When art's abused inventions were unknown;
Kind nature's various wealth was all your own:
And benefits were weighed in reason's scales.

—WILLIAM WORDSWORTH

AWAKENING

With the first, bright, slant beam,
Out of the chilling stream
Their cups of fragrant light
Golden and milky white
From folded darkness spring,
To hail their King.

—ROSE TERRY COOK

THE GIFT OF EASTER

Now every sound and every scene
Blends with overtones of green—
The mist, the rain, the sense of knowing,
And the root renewed in growing.

With turnings of months,
With circlings of days
The earth lives again
With flowerings of praise.

—MARJORIE BERTRAM SMITH

For hope is born when lilacs bloom rain-sweet in early spring,
And faith that found an empty tomb can conquer anything!

—HELEN WELSHIMER

A CANTICLE

Once more is the woodland ringing with buoyant mirth;
Once more are the green shoots springing from under-earth;
Out of the gates of glooming, the depths of dole,
  Like a bud unto its blooming,
  Rise thou, my soul!

Once more there are lyrics lifted from all the rills;
Once more there is warm light sifted on God's fair hills.
Out of the slough of sadness, again made whole
  Into the glow of gladness,
  Rise thou, my soul!

Once more the exultant spirit through nature runs;
  Once more from heaven to hear it lean stars and suns.
    Freed from thy wintry prison, seek thou the goal
      Of Christ, the re-arisen,
      My soul, my soul!
      —CLINTON SCOLLARD

$\mathcal{T}$he great Easter truth is not that we are to live newly after death—that is not the great thing—but that we are to be new here and now by the power of the Resurrection; not so much that we are to live forever as that we are to, and may, live nobly now because we are to live forever.—PHILLIPS BROOKS

THE DAY OF RESURRECTION

Now let the heavens be joyful,
Let earth her song begin,
Let the round world keep triumph
And all that is therein;
Let all things seen and unseen,
Their notes in gladness blend,
For Christ the Lord hath risen,
Our Joy that hath no end!
—JOHN OF DAMASCUS

I believe in Christianity as I believe that the sun has risen,
not only because I see it but because by it I see everything else.
—C. S. LEWIS

ASCENSION

It happens through the blond window, the trees
With diverse leaves divide the light, light birds;
Aeengus, the god of Love, my shoulders brushed
With birds, you could say lark or thrush or thieves

And not be right yet—or ever right—
For it was God's Son foreign to our moor;
When I looked out the window, all was white,
And what's beloved in the heart was sure,

With such a certainty ascended He,
That Son of Man who deigned Himself to be,
That when we lifted out of sleep, there was
Life with its dark, and love above the laws.
—DENIS DEVLIN

AN EASTER CAROL

Spring bursts today,

For Christ is risen and all the earth's at play.

  Flash forth, thou Sun,

    The rain is over and gone, its work is done.

    Winter is past

    Sweet spring is come at last, is come at last.

    Bud, Fig and Vine.

   Bud, Olive, fat with fruit and oil and wine.

  Break forth this morn

In roses, thou but yesterday a thorn.

Uplift thy head,

O pure white Lily, through the Winter dead.

Beside your dams

   Leap and rejoice, you merry-making Lambs.

    All Herds and Flocks

    Rejoice, all Beasts of thickets and of rocks.

Sing, Creatures, sing,
Angels and Men and Birds and everything.
All notes of Doves
Fill all our world: this is the time of loves.
—CHRISTINA ROSSETTI

EASTER SONG

The world has come awake and will be lovely soon
With warm sunlight at noon and ripples in the lake.
Now soon the ground will flower and scarlet tulips grow
Down borders in a row all opened in an hour;

For where the earth was brown the pointed leaves of green
Reach out, and there are seen red flowers folded down:
The snows have gone away and the little birds
Sing songs that need no words, for this is Easter Day.
—MARGARET WIDDEMER

BIOGRAPHIES

of selected poets

BLISS CARMAN (1861–1929) Canadian poet born in Fredericton, New Brunswick.

ELIZABETH COATSWORTH (1893–1986) American poet and author of novels and children's books born in Buffalo, New York. Author of the Sally books and *The Cat Who Went to Heaven*.

DENIS DEVLIN (1908–1959) Irish poet, translator, and diplomat born in Scotland.

EMILY DICKINSON (1830–1886) American poet born in Amherst, Massachusetts. Only two of her over two thousand poems were published during her lifetime.

ELEANOR FARJEON (1881–1965) English author of fiction and short stories, poet, and playwright.

GILES FLETCHER (1588–1623) English poet. Influenced by the poems of Spenser and influenced the writings of Milton.

MARY WESTON FORDHAM (1862–?) American poet. Introduction to her only book, *Magnolia Leaves*, written by Booker T. Washington.

FRANCES FROST (1905–1959) American poet and author born in St. Albans, Vermont. Author of *Innocent Summer*.

A. E. HOUSMAN (1859–1936) English poet and classical scholar born in Frockbury, Worcestershire. Professor of Latin at University College in London and Cambridge University.

JOHN OF DAMASCUS (700?–754?) Theologian, scholar, and writer born in Damascus.

JOYCE (ALFRED) KILMER (1886–1918) American poet born in New Brunswick, New Jersey. Killed during World War I.

CHARLES KINGSLEY (1819–1875) English clergyman, author, and poet born in Devonshire.

LUCY LARCOM (1824–1893) American author, poet, editor, and educator born in Massachusetts. Collaborated with Whittier on several projects.

MARY A. LATHBURY (1841–1913) American author of juvenile fiction and hymnist born in Manchester, New York.

CHARLES GODFREY LELAND (1824–1903) American journalist and humorist born in Philadelphia, Pennsylvania. Author of *A Dictionary of Slang*.

HENRY WADSWORTH LONGFELLOW (1807–1882) American poet, translator, and professor born in Portland, Maine. Published more than fourteen volumes of poetry.

JAMES RUSSELL LOWELL (1819–1891) American poet, essayist, and diplomat born in Cambridge, Massachusetts. Appointed first editor of the *Atlantic Monthly*, and minister to Spain and to England.

GEORGE MACDONALD (1824–1905) Scottish novelist and poet born in Huntly, Aberdeenshire. Wrote a number of children's stories including *The Princess and the Goblin* (1872).

CLAUDE MCKAY (1890–1948) American poet and novelist born in Jamaica. A major figure in the Harlem Renaissance.

DAVID MACBETH MOIR (1798–1851) Scottish physician, poet, essayist, and author. Contributed to *Blackwood's Magazine*.

JOHN RICHARD MORELAND (1880–1947) American poet.

ANGELA MORGAN (?–1957) American poet born in Washington, D.C. Author of "The Unknown Soldier," the poem read over the bier of the unknown soldier in the rotunda of the Nation's Capitol.

LOUISE CHANDLER MOULTON (1835–1908) American poet born in Pomfret, Connecticut.

JOHN G. NEIHARDT (1881–1973) American poet born in Sharpsburg, Illinois. Poet Laureate of Nebraska (1921–1973).

LAURA E. RICHARDS (1850–1943) American author of juvenile fiction, poet, and biographer born in Boston, Massachusetts. Awarded Pulitzer Prize in 1916.

CHRISTINA ROSSETTI (1830–1894) English poet born in London. Author of *Goblin Market and Other Poems*.

MARGARET SANGSTER (1838–1912) American writer and poet. Editor of *Harper's Bazaar* from 1889 to 1899.

CLINTON SCOLLARD (1860–1932) American poet and educator born in Clinton, New York.

HARRIET PRESCOTT SPOFFORD (1835–1921) American author, poet, and essayist born in Calais, Maine.

JOHN BANNISTER TABB (1845–1909) American poet and clergyman born in Amelia Court House, Virginia.

CELIA THAXTER (1835–1894) American writer, poet, and gardener born in Portsmouth, New Hampshire.

JAMES THOMSON (1700–1748) Scottish poet and dramatist.

CHARLES HANSON TOWNE (1877–1949) American poet, author, and editor of *Harper's Bazaar* (1926–1931).

HENRY VAUGHAN (1622–1695) English poet born in Wales. Wrote metaphysical poetry which influenced Wordsworth.

HELEN WELSHIMER (1900–1954) American author, poet, and journalist born in Canton, Ohio.

WILLIAM WORDSWORTH (1770-1850) English poet born in Cockermouth, Cumberland. Poet Laureate of England from 1843–1850.

INDEX BY AUTHOR

INDEX BY TITLE